SURVIVING 30 DAYS OF NOVEL NOVEMBER

HOW TO GET THROUGH A MONTH-LONG WRITING CHALLENGE WITH YOUR SANITY AND SENSE OF HUMOR (HOPEFULLY) INTACT

CARO KINKEAD

To Mom and Dad
who encouraged their writer child

and for Fred,
who believed, even when I didn't

WHERE DID THE IDEA OF "NOVEL NOVEMBER" COME FROM?

2002 found me in a writing slump. I had a string of finished manuscripts, along with a pile of encouraging rejections, but I was burned out, more worried about the best way to "write to market" than putting words on the page. When a friend mentioned this thing called National Novel Writing Month where you tried to write as much of a novel as you could during November. I decided to give it a try in hopes of getting the creativity moving again.

I crashed and burned big time, finishing nowhere near my goal. Part of it was the writing muscles not being warm, part of it the chaos of an auto accident two-thirds of the way through the month (we were fine; the car was not). But taking part did one very important thing: the words started flowing again. Over twenty years later, those thirty days of focusing on my writing have become a ritual.

A lot's changed in that time. I'm self-published and write full-time after leaving the corporate world. The organization which started this madness is no more, but many folks still gather in November to accept the challenge of pushing themselves to write as fast as they can.

The original challenge was to write 50,000 words on a new project, not starting before midnight on November 1 and finishing before 11:59 PM on November 30. This required an average of 1,667 words per day, a daunting task since at that time, I found 1,000 words an outstanding day. The idea was to write like the wind, not stopping for revisions or editing, letting the words flow onto the page. There were no rules as to genre, only that you get to the keyboard and not wait for "someday."

Now, groups organize their own challenges with their own goals, but it's still a roller coaster ride and not everyone's cup of tea. I find the month a way to challenge myself as a writer, and the discipline of hitting that daily goal can have long term effects on your ability to draft more quickly.

What This Book is About

There is no "right" way to do Novel November, as this month is now often referred to, which is part of the appeal. There are, however, any number of wrong ways. When I say "wrong," I'm talking about working yourself into exhaustion, becoming stressed, frustrated, and generally not having a good time. Writing is difficult by nature; why make things worse?

This is not a book to give you tips and tricks on how to "win" your particular challenge. The only guaranteed method I know is to sit your butt in the chair every day for 30 days and work on the goal you're committed to. What I hope to offer is help, support and strategies to make the experience more enjoyable, no matter how much you get done. I've seen far too many people stress out about trying to hit word or page counts to the point where they can't write at all. Trust me, it is not a place you want to be.

Easy to say we should love what we're doing, that writing is supposed to be "fun." It can be, but all too often the work can be a painful slog, an exercise where you'd rather be anywhere but facing that blinking cursor. That's when you need a little encouragement (or a whole lot) because while it's fun to have written, the journey there often resembles a bad remake of *Planes, Trains and Automobiles*.

We're all about the journey here. Let's get ready.

There is a section on preparing for November 1. While I'm seeing more groups organized in spring and summer, November seems to be when most people choose to participate. Habits die hard.

Then, beginning with October 31 and for each day of November, you'll find a brief quotation and some thoughts to make you smile or help you over the bumps that lie along the road. There are other essays as well, focusing on a particular aspect you might encounter. Because Thanksgiving is tied to the fourth Thursday of the month here in the US and not a date, there is a separate entry for that and the day after you can read as appropriate. Once November is over, we'll talk about December, the hangover, and what comes next.

Rules of the Road

The first edition of this book listed the "official" rules:

- Start a new story on November 1
- Write like a whirlwind

- Reach 50,000 words
- Validate your word count on or before November 30
- Collect your winner goodies
- Have fun.

Sounds easy, doesn't it?

Now, the rules will depend on the group whose challenge you take up, but I have a few more suggestions. (It wouldn't be a book of advice if I didn't, would it?)

1. *Show up at the page.* I'm shamelessly stealing this from Julia Cameron and *The Artist's Way*, but this is some of the best writing advice I know. Or, as Nora Roberts has said on a few occasions, "Butt in chair, fingers on keyboard." In all seriousness, while it seems obvious you should write, you'd be surprised how easy it is to say, "I'll do my words tomorrow." One day becomes two becomes three becomes four — and suddenly you're staring down Thanksgiving with just your opening done. Maybe. So, unless there is some dire emergency, commit to that daily word count. Tell yourself it's just for thirty days and you can stop when the month is over.

2. *Don't edit what you've written.* This is key. The point is the forward momentum writing thirty days in a row provides. Don't look back; that's what revision is for. That's for January. **Please note:** If your particular challenge is to revise an existing work, ignore this rule.

3. *There are many roads to Oz.* I have plenty of advice in this book, all of which is based on how I write and the process I follow. My process is not your process, so if something I say runs directly counter to what you do, feel free to take what helps and leave the rest behind.

4. *Don't be afraid to try something new.* If you're a pantser—someone who leaps gleefully into the abyss and writes their story by the seat of their pants—try outlining a little more. If you plot like mad, try writing a story where you dive into the unknown. Write out of order—or in a straight line if you hop around. Let yourself experiment to see if there's something that can help you in your writing process once the month is over.

5. *It's not the end of the world as we know it.* Yes, commit to the page, but don't tie yourself in knots so badly that you can't produce. I'll talk more about not hitting the mark later on but remember that every word you write is a word you didn't have before. Even if you don't make your goal, there are lessons to be learned—and sometimes the best lessons come from not achieving what we set out to do.

Enough rules. On to the details.

OCTOBER

There is no short cut to achievement. Life requires thorough preparation—veneer isn't worth anything.

— GEORGE WASHINGTON CARVER

COMMITTING TO DOING THIS CRAZY THING

I'd love to write, but I never seem to have the time. I certainly don't have time in November, when there's Thanksgiving and all those family commitments. Why can't we do that in a month that's more convenient?

— ALMOST EVERYONE WHEN THEY FIRST
HEAR ABOUT NOVEL NOVEMBER

Let me make a confession here and now—I've used writing in November as an excuse to escape from family gatherings for years. "We'd love to come, but I have to get my words done." Even when I've had to attend the obligations, I've brought a notebook or tapped away on my phone. (Technology is a beautiful thing, especially when it syncs like it's supposed to.)

Yes, November can be a horrible month. There's all the prep for Thanksgiving, the start of prep for Christmas/Hannukah/Kwanzaa/Solstice/Saturnalia/Winter Holiday of Your Choice, and the beginning of End of Year at corporate jobs.

You barely have time for all your obligations, much less add writing or editing words on top of that. What type of crazy person would think adding a writing goal is a good thing?

::And there is a great silence as many people raise their hands, including myself and likely you, dear reader::

Over the years, I've come to believe that November is a great time *because* it's so busy. Think about it—if you can write 50,000 words on a new project or get revisions done, what's to stop you from doing the same thing during the other ten months of the year when you don't necessarily have so many obligations piling up? (We don't talk about December. There's pushing the edge of the envelope and then there's madness. Some folks do accomplish it, brave souls.)

Carving Out Time

So how do you do it? Thanks to technology, getting a few words in during odd moments is a lot simpler than what I began. The first year, I had two choices: either I was chained to my desktop computer or I wrote by hand and transcribed later. If I managed to steal some time at work, writing was accomplished by files sneakily transported via floppy disk, leaving as small a digital footprint as possible. I was a few years from affording my first laptop and smart phones didn't hit the market until a few years after that. iPads and other tablets? That was almost a decade away.

I'm not trying to give you the old "walk up hill two miles to school both ways" speech. If you're determined, you'll write, even if it's scribbling notes on the back of grocery receipts. But technology makes things easier. This book was written on my desktop, my laptop, my iPad, and my iPhone, the files syncing back and forth. It wasn't always smooth, but that ability let me get words in when I had a moment or two —including while waiting for a table at what used to be the Cove Bar in Disney's California Adventure when drafting the first edition. Even if you don't have a tablet or laptop or aren't comfortable typing chunks of text on your phone, pen and paper are still a great way to scratch out story notes or bits of dialogue or description so they don't float away.

You have the tools, but you're trying to find the time in an already packed schedule. The first piece of advice I hear is usually, "Set your alarm clock a half hour earlier, get up and write." Works for some folks, but not others. If you're a morning person and you can get up that half hour earlier, then go for it. But what if you're a night owl, and getting up a half hour earlier would only result in gibberish you'd hate when you were awake enough to read it? I'm all for shitty first drafts, but incoherency often makes a writer feel hopeless. We don't want hopeless.

If you're someone whose mind clicks better in the evening, reverse the process. Either go to bed a half hour later or maybe stop watching television a half hour earlier. See if you can time slip the shows you watch until the weekend and sit down in front of the computer instead. Streaming services that serve up a network's shows the day after airing are helpful. If you're a parent, it'd probably be easier to write when the kids have gone to bed and the house is quiet, even if only for an hour or thirty minutes. Every word you get in during that time is one more word you didn't have before.

Write on your tablet or laptop at lunch. Type a hundred words in on your phone during a break at work—or another bit of dialogue while waiting in line at the supermarket.

Find the odd moments that work for you, even as you're trying to carve bigger moments out of your day. In many ways, the little moments are how you chip away at the big ones.

When you can get twenty minutes, see if a fellow writer is online and would like to do a sprint. Several sprints where you bang out a hundred, two hundred or five hundred words gets you that much closer to your goal.

And there are going to be days when you can't write. If a crisis hits with the kids and school or a crunch time at work, you're going to have to lay the writing aside momentarily. Several times as we were caretaking for my late father-in-law, I spent six hours in the emergency room due to a crisis and the rest of the day dealing with the aftermath. I did write—but only about fifty words. Those words? Got over-written the next morning because my mind wasn't in the game when I put them down. I'll talk more about those days you just can't write later on, but the message is to take care of yourself first. Carving out time does no good if you work yourself to the point of collapse.

Support from Family and Friends

You need some type of support network, folks who will encourage and help you. One of the joys of writing groups on the internet is being a part of the community even as we type away individually. Writing is a solitary craft, but for November, it...isn't.

But fellow writerly types aren't the only ones to cheer you on during this journey. In fact, they're not even likely the main ones. Your main supporters—the ones who'll be impacted the most by your decision to put your writing first and foremost during November—are your family and close friends.

If at all possible, you should get their buy-in. Explain what you're doing and stress this is important to you. If you are the household's main cook, sit down with your partner and come up with a plan to help minimize the time you spend in the kitchen. Talk with your children if they're old enough to understand, let them know there will be times where you need to not be disturbed if possible. Bribery is most definitely an option in this situation and a possibility not to be ignored.

Friends might prove more difficult, but good, true friends will understand you've got things going on for the next month. Let them know that if there is a genuine emergency, you'll be there for them (What just happened on their favorite TV show does not fall into that category) and you'll be eager to spend time with them once the month is done.

Doing this will change the rhythm of your household. You'll quickly realize what shifts don't work—but also keep an eye open for what's a genuine issue and what are sulks over "this isn't the way things usually go and I don't like that."

Dealing with Naysayers

There will be folks who think you're crazy for trying to do this, trying to convince you you're doomed before you even start. Don't listen to them. Remove the negativity from your life!

I can see you rolling your eyes. Seriously, I can, because I've rolled them myself. There are people you can easily ignore if they say you shouldn't do this, that you're a fool for trying—but those are people whose advice you probably already ignore. That's what the "block" and "mute" buttons are for on social media.

When the people saying you shouldn't or you can't are closer than acquaintances? That's a little harder.

I'm incredibly lucky. My husband is supportive of my writing and always has been. But I've been in the other place, too. My late father-in-law sulked each year when he realized it was November and I was not available to instantly respond to his whims. Not *needs* (see earlier comments about ER visits). Whims.

If there is someone close to you who will do their best to rain on your parade, do what's best for *you*. My first instinct is to not tell them what you're doing, which is easier with a friend than family. You can tell them when you're done—or maybe not mention it at all. Remember, you're doing this for yourself, first and foremost. If letting someone know that you've committed to spend November writing is going to cause a fight, don't. It is not worth the time and energy.

There will always be people who will be more than happy to tell you that you can't accomplish something. Ignore them if you can, avoid them if you must. If you've got someone in your life who does that constantly, go to your coping mechanism, but protect your work, your time, your sense of self. Creativity can be a fragile thing. Not because we are *artistes*, but because it is ephemeral, existing only in our imaginations until we bring it to life on the page. And because of this, the spell can be shattered far too easily.

Preparation

Preparation for November is divided into two phases. First is the noveling portion—deciding what you'll be working on, setting your goal, etc. The second is just as important. That is your mental and physical preparation. Committing to Novel November can be wonderful, but also stressful. You can soar to heights of word counts you thought were impossible—but find yourself so wrung out you can't write a word once you're done. We've already talked about the obvious, carving out time, getting support from your family, dealing with folk who aren't going to be supportive. In this section we're going talk logistics to help you make it through the month without being too frazzled. (I will not promise you *won't* be frazzled; I've done this too often.)

Facing The Blank Page

The traditional "rule" is you don't start before midnight on November 1, and when you do, you are facing a blank page. You're allowed to take notes, do outlines and discovery work, but you're not allowed to actually write the *story*.

There are advantages to this method, mainly a clean start with all the possibilities in the world before you. You're not carrying over baggage from a project that wasn't working and there is something about a blank page that is exciting.

It's also frightening. I personally hate the blank page because I'm worried I'm going to get ten or twenty pages in, something will happen and I won't come back to the project. Many of us have such fragments lingering on our hard drives or in notebooks. But if you never start, you'll never finish.

If you're in the middle of an existing project or facing a deadline, set your own goals, but play fair; only those words you write in November should count toward your total. Are you a writer of short stories, not novels? Write two during the month and combine the word count. Know you can't make 50,000 but really want/need to get 25,000 done? Set that as your goal and celebrate when you hit it. If revisions are on the table, set a goal that isn't words, but how far you want to progress with edits in the next thirty days.

This is the big advantage of the challenges shifting from a firm 50,000/new project, as what you need to accomplish will vary year to year. Take a serious look at where you are and what you need to achieve this November. Let that be your guide.

NESTING

Aside from speaking with whomever might share in food preparation at your place, checking out the menus on delivery apps, and deciding what to write, there are a few other things you can do for yourself as November 1 approaches.

1. *Stock up on your favorite office supplies.* You'll need to take notes at some point or keep a journal on what's happening or just have something on hand to doodle on while you think. I've met only a few writers who weren't giddy about office supplies in some way. So, treat yourself: hit the store and buy some pens, markers, stickers or sticky flags. Buy a pack of index cards in different colors or sticky notes you can post on your monitor. Splurge on a new journal. Have some fun.

2. *Clean Up Your Workspace.* Some of you don't need this advice because you always keep the area

where you write straight and uncluttered. I will say officially that I hate you. (No, I don't—but I am envious.) For the rest of us, time to clear away those piles of things which mysteriously migrate to our desk. You know what I'm talking about. The old index cards from a prior project, sticky notes that we no longer need but haven't pulled down, the dust bunnies you've been studiously ignoring. Take some time to tidy everything. You'll be spending a lot of time in this space over the next month (and probably won't tidy again until it's done).

3. *Check your home ergonomics!* The original edition omitted this advice. Pinched nerves and aching muscles weren't big considerations for Past Me, nor was my work area set up in any way that resembled "proper" ergonomics. If possible, make certain your home writing space is as conducive as possible to comfort during for a session lasting multiple hours. Use books to raise your monitor to the correct height for you if necessary. Add/remove pillows to help your posture while sitting. You may need to add a footrest, so your feet are not dangling. There are various sites around the web to help you determine the best configuration without having to break the bank buying new furniture. Future You will be grateful.

4. *Stand regularly.* If you can't adjust your workspace as much as you would like, stand for a minute at least once an hour. Stretch and work out the kinks because you will stiffen up if you're

sitting too long. This is especially useful if you're working in a coffee shop or some other environment where you have to take what you get as far as seating. Again, Future You will be grateful.

5. *Lay in a supply of healthy snacks.* When I was younger, I could keep a small supply of jellybeans by my typewriter and munch on those when I needed to think. Now, I keep unsalted nuts or apple slices nearby. Pick something you will feel okay about mindlessly snacking on (because it will become mindless at some point).

6. *Hydrate!* If you allow your body to dehydrate even slightly (easier than you'd think), focus becomes more difficult, and you'll find yourself tired when you finish a writing session. Fill a travel mug and keep it nearby so you can drink from it mindlessly. If you're at a coffee shop, both coffee and tea will serve, though best to stay away from too many fancy sugary foofy drinks. Besides, if you're occupying a table, it's only polite to buy something for the use of the space. This is a requirement at some establishments.

7. *Timeshift your regular TV viewing (optional).* These days, it's easy to watch your favorite show when it's convenient for you, thanks to streaming services or a DVR. Watching an episode or two is a great (and cost-effective) reward for making your daily goal or hitting a major milestone. It can also be a way to refill the well and let the mind rest, something you also need to be mindful of.

8. *If you're shifting your schedule to gain more writing time, start now.* When folks say to set your alarm to a new time, they don't bother to mention that getting out of bed the first few times are often difficult. Do yourself a favor and shift the schedule prior to November 1. It will be much easier for you to deal with if you allow your body some time to get used to the change. Don't necessarily make the change all at once, either. Set the alarm back five or ten minutes for a few days, then shift it back another few minutes. Repeat until you hit the desired new setting. Much gentler on the body.

9. *Devise a back-up strategy.* Hard drives crash, flash drives fail, phones and tablets can unexpectedly turn into bricks. Back up your work on a daily basis at the very least — and have more than one place where you can store a weekly backup. The odds are technical disaster won't strike during November, but better safe than sorry.

The idea with all of this is to be kind to yourself. You're about to embark on a great adventure and a good, productive writing session can leave you exhausted, both mentally and physically. You can come up from the computer feeling as if you've just run a 400-meter race, though, sadly, writing doesn't burn quite the same number of calories. (If it did, I'd still have those jellybeans by my desk.)

In some senses, you're packing for a trip. Use October to make certain everything is ready—and that you haven't forgotten your toothbrush.

HALLOWEEN AND KICK-OFF

*An intense anticipation itself transforms possibility into reality;
our desires being often but precursors of the things which we are
capable of performing.*

— SAMUEL SMILES

And, suddenly, it's here. October 31. Halloween. The day before. You can feel it, can't you? There's still parties and Trick-or-Treating and last-minute runs to the store for candy and all the other things people do on this day if they celebrate. Enjoy that. If you've got children, take them out, and if you're at home, have a bowl of treats waiting by the door. For me, the giving of candy and exclaiming over costumes adds a very festive air to the proceedings and helps put me in an "up" mood.

Once the children have departed and there's nothing left in the bowl except a few pieces (and the extra bag you bought "just in case"—I'm not judging), time to make one last check of your preparations. Give your writing space a final tweak so it is ready and waiting for you in the morning or at midnight if you can stay up that late. Even if you hang in only long enough to type "Chapter One" and a single sentence, it's a nice feeling to know you have begun.

However you mark it, the moment is finally here. We've anticipated and prepared. Now, let's do this thing.

NOVEMBER

Start by doing what's necessary; then do what's possible; and suddenly you are doing the impossible.

— FRANCIS OF ASSISI

WEEK 1

Beginnings are always messy.

— JOHN GALSWORTHY

NOVEMBER 1

My pencils are sharp enough. Even the dull ones will make a mark.

— ZE FRANK

We love beginnings—a fresh start, a blank page, a moment when all our screw-ups and times we didn't finish don't count. The moment is here, and possibilities lie endless before us.

But beginnings are terrifying as well. The blank page can choke us, make us remember those times when things didn't go as hoped. We go through little rituals, to inspire and get the juices flowing—but also as a way of delaying the inevitable moment when we must begin.

Ze Frank's "Invocation for Beginnings" has become one of my writing rituals, and something I turn to almost any time I feel stuck beginning a project. Available on YouTube, there are also numerous transcripts on the internet. So much of what he says resonates, especially today as the madness starts.

We're looking at a big monster here. We're committing to writing or editing a large chunk in just thirty days. How many times have you said you're going to write X number of words — only to fall far shorter than you'd like?

Let me realize that my past failures at follow-through are no indication of future performance. They're just healthy little fires that'll warm up my ass.

There's been a few bad years in there where these 30 days have been the thing that's kept me going. Thirty days of commitment that get me to the next page, the next paragraph, the next word. Sometimes I announce, "I'm not doing it this year," and my husband gives me that look, the one that says he's humoring me because he knows I'll be in front of the keyboard on November 1.

If my FILDI (Fuck it, let's do it) is strong, let me keep him in a velvet box until I really, really need him. If my FILDI is weak, let me feed him oranges and not let him gorge himself on ego and arrogance.

We make certain our work area is just so or take ourselves off to our favorite coffee shop, avoiding the moment we turn to the blank page or look at the blinking cursor.

And when I get that feeling in my stomach —you know the feeling of all of the sudden you get a ball of energy and it shoots down into your legs and up into your arms and tells you to get up and stand up and go to the refrigerator and get a cheese sandwich — that's my cheese monster talking. And my cheese monster will never be satisfied by cheddar, only the cheese of accomplishment.

Do your rituals, but don't forget what the rituals are for: to signal that we start. It is November 1st and the month lies before us, rife with possibilities.

May your FILDI be stronger than your Cheese Monster.

NOVEMBER 2

All our dreams can come true—if we have the courage to pursue them.

— WALT DISNEY

You made it through Day One, which is sometimes the hardest thing in the world to do. You showed up at the page and created that first chip in your goal. Good for you.

I'm not enamored of the idea of writer as *artiste*, someone who waits for the fragile and fickle muse to bless them with fairy dust in order for the words to flow. Sure, I've got a muse, who eats the chili cheese fries I can't and takes off on vacation whenever the mood strikes her. If I waited for her to bless me with her particular form for fairy dust (which might be hot sauce, given her taste), this book would still be lingering on my computer.

November is about the butt in the chair, working at getting the writing done. It takes effort, and if we want this, we'll make the effort because that's where we choose to put our energy. (Or feel compelled to; writing can be an obsessive thing at times.)

One day down, 29 more to go. Your dreams are worth it.

NOVEMBER 3

Do not let what you cannot do interfere with what you can do.

— JOHN WOODEN

I want all the yarn and to knit all the socks, shawls and sweaters that catch my eye. I want the stories and characters that dance in my head to come to life on the page **right now**.

I want all sorts of things, so many that sometimes I feel as if I will crumble beneath the weight of those desires. So much to do, and, no matter how we want to ignore it, a sure and steadily decreasing supply of time. No matter how hard I work, I will never tell all those stories or knit all the patterns. This is a fact, and no amount of wishing will make it otherwise.

What I *can* do is show up at the page, tell as many stories as I can, even if I'm the only one who ever sees some of them. I can knit to relax and help refill the well, creating objects for myself and those I care for. It's on me to do this, to make the most of what I can do and not let the specter of what might be beyond my grasp hold me back. That's what this November insanity is about; letting go and seeing what I can do.

This is about not settling for "one day" or "when I have time." We never have enough time, no matter how much we live it to the fullest. All we can do is live each day the best we can and decide what's important to us. That's what we need to make time for. We also need to realize our priorities can change, and it's okay to take this time for ourselves, to make that a priority.

Today, let's make it about the words we write.

NOVEMBER 4

*There are people who put their dreams in a little box and say,
Yes, I've got dreams, of course I've got dreams. Then they put the
box away and bring it out once in a while to look in it, and yep,
they're still there.*

— ERMA BOMBECK

In 2009, I came face to face with one of my youthful dreams.
I was in London and stood outside the National Theatre,
where, in my younger days, I'd hoped to tread the boards,
following in the footsteps of Olivier, Patrick Troughton,
Maggie Smith, and many others. At that moment, I could
genuinely taste regret for a dream which disappeared the
moment I decided to move west instead of east. I hadn't realized it then, of course, caught up in the adventure of striking
out on my own. In fact, I thought I was supporting my
dream by seizing a chance to head for Los Angeles *now*
instead of waiting until *then* when plans to move to New
York could come to fruition.

Intellectually, I know that even if I'd gone east, turned left instead of right, it didn't mean I'd have achieved that dream. I've lived in Los Angeles too long to think such things come easily—unless the plot depends on it, of course. But at that moment, standing in front of that building, the box came out. I looked at the dream I'd held close for so long and said goodbye.

Now, I know this doesn't sound particularly inspirational, but sometimes honoring our dreams means admitting we've passed the moment when a particular one can come true. Because if we don't, then it's far too easy to miss the chance to achieve others, our eyes turned from where they need to be. Don't be that person. Don't trade what can be for clinging to what could have been. It's a choice we have to make for ourselves, but if you're involved in this November insanity, then take the time to look at what you're doing, what you wish you could be doing—and what you're willing to work your butt off for, no matter what. Go after that. Chase it.

But realize it's always going to be something you'll be pursuing, because once you catch it and put it in a little box, the dream becomes not what could be, but what could have been.

Go. Chase things.

NOVEMBER 5

Do, or do not. There is no 'try.'

— JEDI MASTER YODA

Yoda was full of it.

There are plenty of times when the only thing we can do is try, even knowing we will look ridiculous, fall flat on our faces, and get something on our clothes that won't come out in the wash. But the thing we are set on is so important to us that we're determined to try anyway.

Of course, if you look at the context in which Yoda utters those words, Luke is defeated before he even begins. His shoulders slump and there's a whine in his voice—the same whine you heard in *Star Wars** when he said he wanted to go into Tosche Station to pick up some power converters. Even when he starts, he swears it can't be done at the first sign of failure.

Luke's looking at the size of what he's being asked to do and thinking Yoda's crazy. It's ridiculous to think anyone can lift an X-Wing out of a (possibly toxic) bog and set it safely on dry land with just the power of the mind. It's not rational and nothing any sane person would attempt. He's not committing to it, and until he commits, he's not able to feel the Force flowing through him.

That's what we're doing right now. We're committing for thirty days even with holidays and family and all the other craziness that goes with November. We'll make the goal or not, but we'll do the writing instead of just thinking about it. And somewhere along the line, we realize Yoda's not talking about effort but intent.

Annoying when he's right, isn't it?

I DON'T CARE that the scroll now reads "Chapter Four: A New Hope." It was simply "Star Wars" when I first saw it and that's what I'll always know it as. Now get off my lawn, you blasted kids.

NOVEMBER 6

Don't tell people how to do things, tell them what to do and let them surprise you with their results.

— GEORGE S. PATTON

I'm something of a pantser, though I've managed to teach myself to do some planning before jumping off the noveling cliff. Still, there's plenty of room for surprise and I have a hero in one book who managed to give me a fun one. He was explaining to his father exactly why he didn't want to go into the family business, and as I typed, I couldn't help thinking he was starting to sound too good and too noble. I'm talking boring good and noble, the type that might make the heroine—and the reader—go seeking a much more entertaining fellow.

Then his father responded to the impassioned speech

with, "Do you have any idea what a pretentious, self-indulgent, entitled imbecile you sound like?"

No, not what I'd been expecting, and it took the scene off in a completely different direction. It also opened up a whole set of possibilities for that relationship which resonated through the book. None of it planned, none of it anything I knew would happen before my fingers moved across those keys.

And that's the fun of it. We write first for ourselves, telling the stories we want to read but no one has written yet. We have the joy of discovery, learning bits and pieces we didn't know existed until they happen. Some will make it into the final manuscript while others will be discarded along the way. We have that joy, though, and that's a reason to put ourselves through this, whether we take 30 days or 300.

Write. Discover something wonderful today.

NOVEMBER 7

Inspiration exists, but it has to find you working.

— PABLO PICASSO

We've made it a week. If everything has gone well, you should reach just under 25% of your goal. If things have gone really well, then you should have a comfortable pad for that day where you will, inevitably, not write a word. Do not panic; it's natural for that to happen and it doesn't have to derail you as long as you show up to the page the day after that.

If things haven't been going well and you're already behind, don't panic. First, we're early enough in the game you can make up that lost ground. Find someone to do some sprints with. A ticking clock can sometimes produce amazing results. Second, don't let yourself walk away from the page. That doesn't mean sitting in front of your computer and beating yourself up because the words won't come. Take a walk. (It's good for you.) Work on your

Christmas knitting. (How many socks did you decide to try for this year?) Do something that will let your mind drift a little.

Think about your story. Try saying a bit of dialogue out loud. If you're out walking, you can use your mobile phone, so it looks like you're in the middle of a conversation. Play with the shape of the words. Remember, if they're not on the page, you haven't fully committed and they're still malleable.

The point of this is to be open to inspiration when it appears. You'll know the moment when it happens; your fingers will start itching and you'll want to get back to that keyboard as quickly as you can. If the keyboard isn't available, then you're going to feel the urge to scribble words on whatever surface is available or use your tablet or record a voice memo on the phone to be transcribed later. Some of my favorite ideas have struck while I'm in the shower and the husband is no longer surprised by the sight of me half-naked, dripping wet, frantically scribbling notes.

Build the habit. Be there at the page every day, make the effort whether you reach word count or not. If you do, then it's amazing how easily inspiration knows where to find you. Go. Write.

SPRINTS AND CHALLENGES

How do you write like you're running out of time?

— "HAMILTON" BY LIN-MANUEL MIRANDA

"Non-Stop" is the Act I closer of *Hamilton*, and a song I'll put on repeat when I'm writing. Like "Sing, Sing, Sing" performed by the Benny Goodman Orchestra, there's a driving beat which helps keep my fingers moving. But it's more than that.

For those who don't know the song, it covers the years between the Battle of Yorktown in 1781 and when Alexander Hamilton became the first Secretary of the Treasury in 1789. He wrote an amazing amount of material in those eight years, including 51 essays that form the bulk of *The Federalist Papers*.

He wrote those 51 essays in six months. While conducting a full-time law practice *and* being a representative to the federal Congress. Yes, it's perfectly fine to feel inadequate. I do when I think of it.

When we're participating in Novel November, we write like we're running out of time because we're up against a ticking clock—all while holding down jobs and other responsibilities. There's an incredible sense of urgency which doesn't impact during the rest of the year.

Despite that, there are days in which it's hard to get fired up, especially if we're falling behind. That's where Word Sprints come in.

While one of my first pieces of advice was to try to avoid things such as Facebook and other social media during November because they can be a time sink, they are also some of the best places to go if you need bit of motivation to help get you moving. Pop into one of your writing groups and see if anyone is up for a sprint. Groups located on Discord often have a channel specifically set up for this. How fast can you write in five minutes, 10, 15, 20?

Trust me, the moment when you realize you just did half your required daily word count in twenty minutes is an amazing motivator. Falling behind? Do some sprints. Realize you have only a very limited amount of time to write on any given day? Do some sprints.

Remember, we are writing a shitty first draft here. No one expects you to produce polished prose in these thirty days. (Except, perhaps, non-writers. Ignore them.) The point is to get the words out and get your creativity flowing so you'll have something to work with in revisions.

Go do some sprints. Write like you're running out time.

WEEK 1 WRAP-UP AND LOOKING AHEAD

This week...

- Midnight on November 1 struck and we began!
- There is probably no more Halloween candy in the house. If there is, I applaud your restraint.
- Have you backed up your work?
- Are you logging your words?
- You will (hopefully) have reached approximately 25% of your goal by the end of November 7

NEXT WEEK...

- We drive to the halfway point
- The shininess of beginning wears off and things might feel a bit more of a slog.

WEEK 2

*If you're walking down the right path and you're willing
to keep walking, eventually you'll make progress.*

— BARACK OBAMA

NOVEMBER 8

Have you ever seen a little girl run so fast she falls down? There's an instant, a fraction of a second before the world catches hold of her again...A moment when she's outrun every doubt and fear she's ever had about herself and she flies. In that one moment, every little girl flies. I need to find that again. Like taking a car out into the desert to see how fast it can go, I need to find the edge of me...And maybe, if I fly far enough, I'll be able to turn around and look at the world... And see where I belong.

— "CAPTAIN MARVEL" BY KELLY SUE DECONNICK

A lot of people don't like the idea of a large writing challenge in November because of the complication of Thanksgiving and the start of the annual Holiday Insanity. I welcome it for one very important reason. My birthday marks the beginning of the second week and each year I do this means I spend at least part of the day doing one of the things I love most in the world: writing.

I generally take some time off from the computer during the weekend nearest to the day itself to do something fun—often a film I want to see is opening around this time—but on that day, I will spend as much time as possible in front of my computer, fingers on the keyboard. It's my gift to me, putting myself first in the midst of any other calls for my attention. It's a reminder and affirmation that, yes, this is who I am and what I do, no matter what other roles I play.

Today's quote is from the first issue of *Captain Marvel* (2014), written by Kelly Sue DeConnick, with art by David Lopez and colors by Lee Loughridge, titled, "Higher, Further, Faster, More." Those words, which appear on the issue's final pages, have become something of a mantra among many women in comics fandom. It's a call to find the wonder time and the world has ground out of us, to be more. That's what we're doing here. We're running so fast and we're going to fall down at some point. If nothing else, the month will end and this experience will be done, pulling us back to earth. But if we keep running this month, there will be those moments when we fly.

I wouldn't miss those moments for anything in the world.

NOVEMBER 9

I love deadlines. I especially like the whooshing sound they make as they go flying by.

— DOUGLAS ADAMS

When I was in the corporate world, this time of year found me drowning in whooshing deadlines. These were reliant on folks in other areas and if they came in late, it pushed everything else back—running into some hard deadlines which couldn't be moved. Which meant I often found myself in a last-minute panic.

Even with all this, the writing continued. Notes scribbled in margins during meetings, typed into the phone on the sly. Lunch was my meal and typing into my iPad, making certain in that everything was synced with the desktop computer in the evening, and I hadn't lost any important bits.

I hate pressure. It's the feeling that tightens your shoulders and makes you ache well before the day is done.

Without that pressure, though, there is no sense of urgency, nothing to move you forward. There is no conflict, and just as we're approaching the point where we suffer the annual "My writing sucks!" moment, we need that struggle between us and the calendar to make certain we move forward. If nothing else, deadlines are our signposts along the way.

NOVEMBER 10

Writing is a process, a journey into memory and the soul.

— ISABEL ALLENDE

Arewethereyetarewethereyetarewethereyet?

— BART AND LISA SIMPSON

Energy and enthusiasm seem to carry folks through the first week of November—or any new project, for that matter. The second week is where the thing is no longer quite so shiny and new and is a long way from being finished. Suddenly, sitting down in front of the keyboard or picking up the knitting needles becomes much less enticing. Today, we're supposed to hit 16,667 words for those folks who are aiming for 50K. (If not, your mileage will vary.) It sounds like a lot of words. It is a lot of words.

It's also only one third of the way through the damn process. Twenty days left to go. We tell ourselves it's all about the journey, but there is a part of our brain that's got "Are we there yet?" on permanent loop.

I love writing; it's one of my favorite things in the world. There are also moments when I feel as if I would rather have a root canal without anything to numb the gums than sit at the keyboard and pull the words out of my brain. It is part of the journey, though. You cannot have written without actually writing. And the thing about journeying is that there's always going to be the bit where you're just glad to get through this stretch because the traffic is bad, the terrain's taxing on your car or there are...interesting sights and smells.

But we keep going because we want to reach our destination and we're convinced it's worth the effort. Sometimes it's hard to remember at this point, but we'll make it. Onwards and upward. In the meantime, ignore the two kids in the back seat.

NOVEMBER 11

To see what is in front of one's nose needs a constant struggle.

— GEORGE ORWELL

Ever have one of those moments when you know what you want to write but the words seem just out of reach? They're right there, but...

It's a frustrating feeling, and one I often find myself struggling with. I know I'm supposed to write fast and not let my internal editor get the better of me, but there are moments, especially as I move beyond the big scenes which inspired the story, where the internal editor rears her head, making me second guess my word choice, hit the back button too often and decide that, no, the story really needs to go in a new direction that will necessitate throwing out everything I've already written.

That's what seems so clear and obvious, but what is in front of my nose is that after ten days, it's easy to become distracted and try to edit the story as you tell it. This challenge is not about that. What's needed is to let it go and let the words flow. (Put on the soundtrack from *Frozen* if it helps get you in the mood.)

Once the month is done, step away for a time, then look at your story with an eye toward making sense of the puzzle pieces.

Right now, what we need to focus on is just telling the story, however it falls out.

NOVEMBER 12

If you are going through hell, keep going.

— WINSTON CHURCHILL

Does it feel like a slog yet? For some folks, that comes during Week Three. For others, it starts on Week Two. It's that moment when you look at the words still to go and groan. For me, I know it's going to get more difficult as I start trying to fill in the connective tissue between my major scenes. Those are the worst moments.

But as we see the midpoint drawing closer, we have two options: go forward or give up. We can junk everything we've done to this point. Move the file on your hard drive, delete it, whatever makes you happy. I've done that. One year, I was about halfway through when I told my friends who were also participating (and were the ones who'd dragged me in originally) I wasn't going to make it, the project wasn't working, and it was better for me and my sanity if I just let it go.

There are times when letting go is the right thing to do. It was then, and that idea has never been revisited, unlike a number of others. I didn't make the decision lightly, and only after realizing not only was the story not working, trying to hit my word count was causing so much stress I didn't want to write at all. And not just on the project at hand.

Sometimes, walking away is the best thing one can do. Illness, family crisis, a computer that rolls over and dies, taking your manuscript with it—those are reasons to say, "Not this year." If you're in a position where taking even one thing off your plate can feel as if a huge weight has been lifted from your shoulder, you might want to consider it.

Most of the time, though, it's simply the easiest reaction to resistance, deciding not to do the slog. Of course there's resistance. When you're fried at the end of the day, writing is hard. You'd rather collapse on the couch and watch your favorite television show. I'd rather collapse on the couch and watch my favorite television show; but I also want to watch the word count ratchet up, see myself inch closer to the finish line. Can I finish before the 30th? Can I make more than 50,000 words, get most of an entire first draft finished? These are the thoughts which keep me going when the going gets tough, when it feels like hell and all I want to do is stop.

You're hopefully hitting 20,000 words today or pushing beyond that. Yeah, getting there can be hell. But when you're there, doesn't it feel good?

That's why we keep going.

NOVEMBER 13

My notes are written in blood on the sand, the same as any writer.

— J. MICHAEL STRACKZYNSKI

It'd be so easy to just say "Yup" and move on. I don't think any writer's story has ever turned out exactly the way they imagined it would when they started. Even if your ending is what you imagined, and the big scene in the middle hit all those right notes which came to you like a vision in the shower, it's still not exactly what you thought it would be. Somewhere along the way, you write something and it comes out...different. Maybe it's the heroine's cat or the old friend you didn't know your main character had. Maybe it's an allergy to citrus or a shiver that passes over their skin if they touch raw wood. Maybe it's a minor detail that adds color and maybe it's something that sends everything careening in a different direction you didn't anticipate, but you know this is a thread you must follow.

Since I'm something of a pantser, I can roll with that scenario. Some of my best stuff has come from things I didn't know were going to be there. But I've seen friends who are determined, dedicated plotters faced with the same situation, and often all one can do is feed them chocolate and help them through the panic. Once they make peace with the fact the story insists on going in that direction because their subconscious has made some leap they hadn't anticipated, they're usually much better at figuring out just how deep the rabbit hole goes and are back on track while the rest of us are still digging.

So how do you know if you're on the right track when things start veering wildly? Ask a few questions:

Does it somehow fit with what you've already written? *(A new start for the book or between existing scenes? This could be good.)*

Will adding this cause you to do extensive rewrites to the story while you're in the middle of drafting? *(Not necessarily good, but if you feel really strongly about it, you may decide that's worth the risk.)*

Does this idea have absolutely no connection to anything you've written up to this point and you're going to be leaving all that behind, starting over? ***(Danger, Will Robinson! Danger!)***

Let me confess that while the original intent was to start something new and finish it, I have had years where the story you start to tell really isn't the story you need to be telling at this point. I have dumped a week of work and started fresh with a new idea that was burning in my brain, racing to catch up with my word count. That's usually worked pretty well because the idea hit me so strongly that I had to work on it now or I was going to be unhappy.

I've also been a victim of "Look! Shiny!" on more than one occasion. That's your inner editor talking, teasing you with the thought that what you're not writing is the better idea. We try not to speak of those times in my house.

So how do you know when to leap and when not to? You listen to your gut. There's getting inspiration and there's deciding to jettison a bunch of hard work on a whim. If you stop to think about it and trust yourself, you'll know. Remember, this month is about trusting yourself, and there's no harm in scribbling that brilliant idea down in a notebook and moving on.

Besides, the advantage of notes written in the sand is that it's easy to change things if necessary. Just make sure the tide doesn't come in on you.

NOVEMBER 14

The road to hell is paved with works in progress.

— PHILIP ROTH

It's too damn easy to let life get in the way of the important things, and if one is going to write—really, seriously, "I want to be published and earn money with this" write—then writing must be one of the important things.

Life is a series of choices. Sometimes nothing can stop us and sometimes we put stuff on hold for what are very good, solid reasons at the time. The problem is, getting back to what you put on hold can prove difficult. (Ask any knitter; they probably have loads of unfinished objects they put aside "just for now" that are still lurking in bins. There's a reason Ravelry has the "hibernate" option for projects.)

There have always been those who decry the very idea of the month of writing madness. They say it encourages bad writing, pretends writing is a hobby that can be taken up and put down, pushing the idea novels can be churned out in a month. I've seen some heated blog posts (and heated responses) on the subject and I wonder why some folks are getting themselves so worked up about the idea. If you don't do it, fine. That's your decision.

In the end, we should either do or not do these things for ourselves and if other people decide not to do it, or color outside the lines while participating, what's the big deal? Have fun. Practice some discipline. (Those two statements are not mutually contradictory). We're just a day away from 25,000 words. Even if you're not quite at the mark, look at all the words you have now that you didn't have on October 31. Look at all the days you sat down and made writing important to your daily routine. That, right there, is a major accomplishment to be proud of.

"THAT" DAY

We live in a rainbow of chaos.

— PAUL CEZANNE

You'll know it when it comes. That's the day when nothing seems to work and everything is dissolving into chaos, each task you try falls apart.

We've all had them. We all hate them. We look at others, and it seems as if they never experience such troubles, which only makes us feel worse. Guess what? They do. They just have those doubts where we don't see.

You'll hit that day at some point during these four weeks. It may have been this week, causing you to stumble just out of the gate. It may be near the end of the month as you're desperately trying to get words in, so you'll hit 50,000. Thanksgiving is that day for a lot of people. It's the day when the world seems to conspire to make sure you can't write.

Sometimes, the world wins—and that's just the way of it.

No matter how many streaks you have, how dedicated you are to sitting down in front of that keyboard, things will conspire to prevent you. I'm not talking the mental wall writers can face, but external forces that mean you don't go anywhere near the keyboard for some reason or another. The question is how you'll deal with it.

One way is to write more than your projected word count each day if you can because that gives you a pad, insurance against those days when life intrudes. Some folks get the wind under their wings late in the game because the story has caught fire. Great if it happens and I've seen amazing numbers appearing those last few days each November, but I'm of the school of thought that it's better to write more early as a hedge against the slings and arrows life throws at you.

There's one other thing you can do: get back on the horse tomorrow. If today has been complete and utter crap, if the world's been falling on your head and you didn't have enough time to even glance at your computer or tablet, let it go. Try to get a good night's sleep and try again tomorrow.

We all have those days. The important thing is to know they happen and when they do, *it is not the end of the world.* In 1999, the Dali Lama was asked what he thought would happen when the calendar ticked over to 2000. "The sun will come up. It will be a new day."

The day happens but tomorrow is a new one and a new chance to write. If today is crap, let's seize tomorrow.

WEEK 2 WRAP-UP AND LOOKING AHEAD

This week...

- We moved out of the first moments of enthusiasm and toward the treacherous waters of the middle.
- We may have felt the first tendrils of frustration and the hint of a slog.
- Have you backed up your work?
- Are you logging your words?

NEXT WEEK...

- Halfway there!

WEEK 3

So the lover must struggle for words.

— T.S. ELLIOT

HOW MANY WORDS AM I IN THE HOLE?

Struggling is hard because you never know what's at the end of the tunnel.

— DON RICKLES

Not the cheeriest way to start our third week, but since we're supposed to be hitting the halfway mark on the 15th, it's probably a good time to talk. If all things are going well, you're right at your midpoint, possibly a little bit over or under—but nothing that can't be made up with one good extra-long writing session or maybe a sprint or two.

Let's say things are not going so well, though. Let's say you're a thousand words down. Two thousand. *Five thousand. More.* Time to admit there's a problem. Maybe the book isn't working, maybe life is getting in the way. Maybe it's a confluence of things. Whatever the reason, you need to make choices.

Look at how many words you are behind on word count and decide if this is an amount you can reasonably make up.

Take a look at your calendar and block out any time you can possibly convert to writing time. Go through that and find the moments where you can be certain you can sit down for an hour or two—even just 20 or 30 minutes—and just write. Make yourself appointments for those times, plan to get out of the house if necessary.

Now take the number of words you're behind and divide them by the number of days you have left to write. Five thousand words behind converts to 333 extra words per day. Difficult, but that really is a good sprint or two every single day. Again, see if that's something you can add to your schedule or if you know you're going to have trouble. If you can, focus on the page and get the work done. It's going to take some effort and there is no guarantee you'll cross the finish line with 50,000 words come November 30. But it gives you a plan and hope. (I may be a pantser for my writing, but I've found planning for my writing time is a great help.)

Even if the word deficit seems ridiculous, I urge you to make a plan and give catching up a try. You may not make it, but you'll have more written than you began the month with. However, don't get overly stressed about it all. Yes, that seems like a contradiction in terms, but remember, we're trying to get through November without driving ourselves crazy or putting ourselves in a place where we can't write.

You've got sixteen days to go. Let's make the most of them.

NOVEMBER 15

*You have to accept whatever comes and the only important
thing is that you meet it with the best you have to give.*

Welcome to Week Three. Believe it or not, we're halfway
there. This is the moment where we start to wonder "What
was I thinking?" Maybe it's, "What was I thinking signing up
for this insane thing?" Or maybe it's, "What was I thinking
when I dreamed up this story?"

It's nothing that can't be fixed in editing, but you can get
a little itchy because some of it is just not the way you envi-
sioned things. There's a great urge to slow down and edit.
Cresting the top of the hill and seeing the downward slope,
try to grab hold of the cart and ride this thing all the way
down.

Write with gusto. Write with abandon. Don't be afraid of
what is on the page at this moment. It is all mutable in the
end. You can revise almost anything but let the bones be

what they will be and embrace them. Give it your all. Don't let doubt hold you back or stay your hand from allowing a scene run longer than you know you should. When you edit, you may cut two-thirds of what you've written, but it is also possible there is some gem you would have lost if you didn't let yourself go. A detail, a phrase, a moment which makes your story richer.

That's why we draft. We are building our bones, laying the foundation. Some of it likely won't pass code inspection and we'll have to do major reworks, but if you give your story the best you have to give, even in the reconstruction, there will be things of beauty.

Go forth and write. You're halfway there.

NOVEMBER 16

To err is human. To blame it on somebody else is even more human.

— ARTHUR BLOCH

There are so many things that can keep us from our writing, and this month is full of them, with a big one staring us in the face next week. It's not just Thanksgiving, though; there are constantly things which drag our attention away from the keyboard and our words. Most of us don't have the luxury of writing full time. We carve out bits and pieces from the day, and if the day doesn't go as we hoped or plan, it's often the writing that suffers. And when it does, we have plenty of excuses. We're exhausted from our job, homework needs to be checked, there's some emergency requiring our attention. We let ourselves be talked into doing an article for the church newsletter we didn't really want to write, the committee we get talked into serving on, the series on Netflix we've been waiting for just became available—those are times when we look back, realize we didn't get the writing done and want to place the blame on others for us not doing what we know we should be doing.

There are times when we cannot write, when other things truly need our attention. I don't think anyone expects us to write in the middle of fresh grief, or when life is literally falling apart around you. But it's too easy to let the little difficulties become large roadblocks, to give yourself the excuse to say "tomorrow." We need to take responsibility for our choices and that means owning up to the times we say "yes" when we know we should say "no", or when we kick our feet up and decide to watch TV instead of turning to the keyboard. It's better that way because if we keep making the choice not to write, then maybe we'll start asking ourselves why we're doing that—which possibly points to a bad case of impostor syndrome or something else that's causing us to retreat.

Even if you can't meet your whole goal, try to write something. Every word on the page is a word you didn't have before, and if you write something on a day that's bad, it's easier to write something the next day. Even a paragraph or sentence will do.

Besides, if you really need to vent your frustrations about someone, write that person into your story and do something dreadful to them. You can always edit it out later.

NOVEMBER 17

Fall seven times and stand up eight.

— JAPANESE PROVERB

This is the point where folks start having real difficulty, and we start hearing the words "I'm not going to make it this year." You may be at a point where you feel like saying it yourself. If there's any way possible, don't. Don't look at the words you need to make up as a whole but break it down into manageable chunks. Make it a separate goal, if you have to. Write your daily words and then write 54 separately. Try word wars or sprints to make the most of small bits of time for writing.

We all fall sometimes, but the point is, get back up and try again, to not stay down. Yes, sometimes we need help getting back up and sometimes it hurts and all you really want to do is just stay there and forget you ever tried in the first place. I know that feeling because I've had it. There are days (and weeks and months) where life can suck, and you don't feel it's worth making the effort because you know you're never going to make up the ground you lost.

The thing is, sooner or later, you have to get up. You can get up on your own, or other people or events will physically drag you from where you are to someplace else that is not of your choosing. As much as it can hurt—and it really can hurt, physically, emotionally, mentally—it's better for us to rise on our own. Finish or not, at least we know we made the choice.

Writing is a constant process of falling and standing up again. Plots don't work, characters veer in directions we didn't intend, our carefully constructed house of cards falls to pieces in front of our very eyes. Sometimes we need to walk away from the keyboard for a little while, but we come back, settle our butts in the chair and stand up again on the page.

If you fall, rise again, as many times as are necessary. If you need help, hold out a hand. You'd be surprised how many people are there for you if you ask.

NOVEMBER 18

I think, at a child's birth, if a mother could ask a fairy godmother to endow it with the most useful gift, that gift should be curiosity.

— ELEANOR ROOSEVELT

I was lucky—both my parents let me indulge my curiosity. I grew up surrounded by books, music, film, television, all of which helped feed my imagination. I put on plays with my dolls, had imaginary friends, and was perfectly happy to curl up with a book when the Texas skies would open and going outside wasn't an option.

Curiosity is a wonderful gift and something essential for a writer. In the beginning was the word and the word is "What if?" What if, on the run with the company bankroll, a secretary checks into a creepy motel?

What if the reigning social diva for one small town uproots herself to another?

What if a genius, billionaire, playboy, philanthropist was

kidnapped while overseas and had to invent a device that would help him escape?

What if a girl was hit on the head and went over the rainbow?

What if...

Writers see stories everywhere because we are curious. It is in our nature. The imaginary friends we enjoyed as children are still with us, living in the tales we tell. Even when we're not at the computer, we can often feel them itching under our skin, fingers tingling with the urge to tell one more story. Words are our friends, whether we wrote them or they're part of our favorite books. We are armchair adventurers, living the lives we imagine and want to share.

Look at what we're doing now. We're sitting down and trying to write 50,000 (more or less) words in the space of 30 days, which is crazy in and of itself. But we're also trying to do it in one of the craziest months of the year. Why? Because at some point, we asked ourselves, "What if I can do this?"

Curiosity. It's what brings us here and what keeps us moving and writing. Let's see what surprises it has for us today.

NOVEMBER 19

You can't wait for inspiration. You have to go after it with a club.

— JACK LONDON

Some days, going after something with a club is an almost overwhelming temptation. It could be the person who interrupted you in the middle of a writing sprint when everything was flowing. It can be the day job which seems determined to ensure you can't finish your tasks because other departments don't pass on the information you need when you need it.

For writers, we're reaching the point where it is very often the book we're working on.

This is the danger zone. Everything looks shiny and far more interesting than what you've got going in front of you. Everything is tempting and there's that new idea that's rattling around in your otherwise (feels like) empty brain. All you need to do is take just a little time from what you're supposed to be working on, and you'll get right back, feeling re-energized. How much damage could ten minutes (half an hour, two days, until midnight November 29) working on something else do?

Or you've hit the point where you're convinced that everything you write is crap and folks are on the verge of figuring out you're a complete phony, and the only reason you're insisting on doing this thing is so you have an excuse to not talk to the relatives or linger on Thanksgiving because you have to get words done. You're already wondering what you're going to say when (insert family day of obligation of your choice) comes in December and those relatives you avoid now say, "So, what's happening with that thing you were writing?"

We've got eleven days to go, and we should reach around 63% of our goal by the end of today. If you're there or beyond, great. You know where your inspiration is, your FILDI is strong and unless something upsets the apple cart, you're probably going to be crossing the finish line on the 30th. If you're not, though...

These are the times that try a writer's soul. This is where writing is not fun. It's always fun to have written, but there are moments when it's not fun doing the work. This is where you put your butt in your chair and your fingers on the keyboard whether you want to or not and you get it done. Trust me, you're not going to regret the time you miss on Facebook if you get it done. You will regret the words that didn't get written because they'll itch at you. That's what mine do.

Get your club and hunt yourself some inspiration.

NOVEMBER 20

It is not what you gather, but what you scatter, that tells what kind of life you have lived.

— ANONYMOUS

I'm unfortunately at the age where it becomes increasingly common to learn that someone who's been a part of my landscape has passed away, leaving a hole. Some big, some small, but you hear the news, and the world is different.

Or you open your browser or see the news alert on your phone. Something horrible has happened somewhere. We live in an unsettled age (was any age truly "settled"?) and all too often there is violence, pain, suffering and death. Sometimes it's on the other side of the world and sometimes it is far, far, too close to us.

Every day, we have reminders that our time on this earth is limited, and it is up to us to do the most with the time we've been given. There are moments when the world seems cold and cruel—far too often of late—and the only thing which warms it are those who inspire and bring us joy. Hold on to those close to you and let them warm you, just as you warm them in return. Go out and live life. Be excellent to one another. *Live.*

Tell your story. No matter how far behind you may be, getting those words out, even if you only write them for yourself, is part of the love you make in your life. If doing it gives you joy, then you will give joy to others. We're closing in on the home stretch, so we're not down and out yet.

And, when you have a chance, raise a glass to those who have gone before. When we remember and recount the memories, they live again in our hearts and minds, even if only for that moment.

NOVEMBER 21

The greater danger for most of us is not that our aim is too high and we miss it, but that it is too low and we hit it.

— MICHAELANGELO

It's easy to play it safe, and that's one of the struggles I try to overcome when I'm writing. I do well in a sprint and discover my characters playing so nicely with one another there's no real conflict. There's a problem with this: it's not just boring to read, it's really, really boring to write.

There's a reason this place is called a "comfort zone"; it's where we head naturally. We know the parameters, we know how people are supposed to react and things should turn out. It doesn't stretch us and it's...safe. We don't want to venture out of that defined little area because when we do, we're threatened with failure. It's there nibbling at the edges of our consciousness, letting us know we're taking a risk. Risk is bad. Risk is...risky. So much easier to stay with the tried and true. Except...

We can fail with the tried and true as well because the work no longer has anything behind it except a series of steps that have been locked into place in advance. Step one: Meet Cute. Step Two: Misunderstanding. Step Three: First Kiss. Step Four: Escalating Misunderstanding. Step Five: Slo-Mo Love Scene With Song We Are Hoping Will Become a Pop Hit. Step Six: More Misunderstanding Substituting for Black Moment. Step Seven: Final Clinch and Reprise of Potential Pop Hit. Alternate Ending: Substitute Second Pop Hit Hopeful. Sound familiar?

This month is the time to go outside your comfort zone, let your characters misbehave, act out, do things you would *never* let them do in a draft anyone was going to read beside yourself. Let them be extreme. You can soften some of the rough edges later because that's what revision is for. Not everything we write will be golden. Hell, most of what we write won't be golden. A good deal could probably be used to fertilize the tomato plants. But we should be willing to risk falling from time to time because that's the way we know we're reaching further and further.

We have ten days left. Today, I'm challenging you to let your characters do something outrageous today, just to see how those around them react. The results may surprise you.

THE WELL FEELING DRY—A
CAUTIONARY TALE

When the well is dry we know the value of water.

— BENJAMIN FRANKLIN

There was a day when I sat down at my computer to write an editor's note for a newsletter. Wasn't anything long or demanding of my creativity. Just a few words to say hello and talk about what was in that issue. The thing was, I couldn't. My fingers hovered over the keyboard and... nothing.

We've all felt blocked on one occasion or another, the words refusing to come. It's not fun and makes you want to bang your head against the wall. You take a deep breath, you noodle around, you try to approach things sideways and get the words flowing again. We all have our different methods because we know the words are in there somewhere. What we need is to get them out.

This wasn't that sensation. I tried to write—and there were no words at all, just a hollowed out feeling as if I was missing a piece of myself. After sitting there for another minute, I wandered out into the living room and told my husband, "I have no words." Then I burst into tears.

This might seem a bit melodramatic, but that awful, terrible feeling can happen to any writer. There was a lot going on in my life, my job was ridiculously stressful, I was trying to write while doing a bunch of other things—and I'd let the well run dry. I wasn't reading, I wasn't soaking in that which fuels my creativity, and I wasn't taking care of myself. Up early, to bed late, too many things on my plate and rushing from one task to another.

Sound familiar?

I don't wish that feeling on anyone, but it can happen if we're not careful. After three weeks of pushing yourself to new frontiers of story and word counts, it's very easy to be at the point where what you're working on is pretty much all-consuming, which means you're pulling a lot of creative energy from that well. And because you are so focused there, you don't stop to make certain you're replenishing your energy. Maybe you have enough to get you through this. Maybe you don't.

This is different from the day where nothing goes right, and you can't get to your keyboard. This is crash and burn big time, where we're not talking maybe putting this year's challenge in jeopardy, but finding yourself in a place where you won't be writing for an extended period because there's nothing left for you to draw on.

Hopefully, you just shudder reading this and move on. If, however, these words strike a chord in you and you can feel that hollow space lurking just out of reach, do yourself a favor. No matter what it does to your word count, step away from the keyboard. Read a book. Knit. Watch television.

Give yourself some time to refill that well with things that stimulate your mind in a different way from writing. Go for a walk, have a lie-in if you can, take your partner out to dinner, or just go sit in a coffee shop and people watch.

No matter how highly we cling to the idea of succeeding, it is not worth pushing yourself into a place where you simply cannot write another word because you don't have another word in you. One is a short-term win; the other can leave lasting damage.

Please, be good to yourself. This month and whenever you're trying to push through some writing, try to add in some time where you can step away from the keyboard and enjoy the things that excite you creatively. You will be the better for it.

WEEK 3 WRAP-UP AND LOOKING AHEAD

This week...

- We crossed the mid-point
- Some may be falling behind in word count, but there is still time to make it up.
- Have you backed up your work?
- Are you logging your words?

NEXT WEEK...

- We're on the downward slope, with the end in sight.
- Thanksgiving is coming! Turkey! Pie! Relatives! Possibly not getting to write at all that day!

WEEK 4

Optimism is the faith that leads to achievement. Nothing can be done without hope and confidence.

— HELEN KELLER

NOVEMBER 22

Writing a book is an adventure. To begin with it is a toy and amusement. Then it becomes a mistress, then it becomes a master, then it becomes a tyrant. The last phase is that just as you are about to be reconciled to your servitude, you kill the monster and fling him out to the public.

— WINSTON CHURCHILL

Welcome to Week Four. The first overachievers are hitting their challenge goal while most of us are still struggling in the wastelands. Hopefully, yours is within sight, along with the knowledge that one week from tomorrow, Novel November will end.

Time to start thinking about what's next. Even before November 1, the ticking clock has been the tyrant driving us forward. Freedom is almost at hand, however. No more check-ins, no more marking your progress against others or where the numbers say you "should" be. The question now becomes, are you going to keep writing and finish the draft?

Are you going to take a breather? How long of a breather? And how long is too long?

Some folks dub December as Novel Revision Month, while others decide December is for finishing the bulk of their draft. I agree with the latter. If you haven't reached "The End" by November 30, keep writing, and start your revisions with the new year.

The point is the process is on-going. Committing to write for a month isn't an end unto itself, but a step along the way. Let's keep moving.

NOVEMBER 23

I'm very proud of my flops, as much as of my successes.

— FRANCIS FORD COPPOLA

I'm going to be writing a lot about failure this week because we are staring down the end of this challenge, and I know some folks are struggling mightily. I will say what other people have probably already told you: keep writing. Every word you write is a word you didn't have on October 31. While "winning" ends at midnight on November 30, there is nothing which says you must stop writing.

The idea behind these thirty days of literary madness is to set yourself free for one month, give yourself permission to write an utterly shitty first draft and just go with the flow. The point of writing a shitty first draft is setting yourself up to fail spectacularly, to write something that you know, when you finish, is not going to be publishable immediately and may not be publishable for a while as you smooth out rough edges, fix the cracks, and perform an earthquake retrofit. Don't worry about quality in these last eight days—just write. Trust your mind to lead you where you need to go and write. Do sprints, find a prompt to get the juices flowing, challenge yourself to write a certain number of words beyond what you'd normally write in a given time. Just let the story happen.

You're not alone in your struggles. I've known more than one November where I made my 50,000 words but were miserable experiences for one reason or another. I'm still proud of participating, because those have happened when my writing and my life were at a very low point. I'm proud because I sat down at the keyboard when I had every reason not to do so. I'm proud of the effort because doing that, remembering those moments when the writing was good and felt right, helped me come back from serious dry spells. It wasn't easy, but it was a baby step.

We learn something from everything we do, success or failure. Many times, it's the failures which hold the greatest lessons because they give us signposts as to what roads we shouldn't go down, warnings the bridge is under construction, and we need to take a detour. Our failures help us not make the same mistake twice in the same way.

If you're close to winning, celebrate because you've earned that right and congrats to you. If you're struggling, plan to celebrate December 1, goal met or no. You made it through the month and even if you fell short, you didn't give up. That's a hell of a lot more than some folks ever do. In the weeks ahead, as you gain time and distance, you can look back at the experience and consider the lessons learned. After that, it's not too early to start thinking about what you plan to write in the coming year.

NOVEMBER 24

If you don't allow yourself the possibility of writing something very, very bad, it would be hard to write something very good.

— STEVEN GALLOWAY

I've won these challenges most of the years I've sat down to do the madness. I love much of what I've written in November. A few years back, I uncovered a Regency romance which was probably one of the easiest wins I've ever accomplished. Unfortunately, the traditional Regency market was dying at that point and while I had some nibbles from editors, it never really stood a chance. I've now revised and self-published, something not even on the horizon when the story was conceived

There are, however, other manuscripts which emerged from my November writing. There's the one that began with fifteen pages of exposition. No matter how hard I tried, my mind couldn't find a way to trim things down because the information didn't fit anywhere else. It didn't fit anywhere else because the structure of the story was fundamentally flawed. There's the one that had more characters than *War and Peace*—and was perhaps one-third the length. Or the one where, when my husband perused the manuscript in December, noted there seemed to be three separate books, none of which had a coherent plot.

These were very, very bad books. Copies are tucked away in a box at the back of the closet because every so often, I feel compelled to pull them out and see if maybe I've learned enough to somehow salvage these wrecks. Every time, they go back in the box and back in the closet.

I did learn things from the writing, though. I learned I need to be ruthless in cutting large blocks of solid text because I tend to run to info dumps. I learned I can handle a scene with more than two characters, but if I have more than four, I need to ask if all those voices are necessary. Also, you don't name everyone who walks onto the stage. I learned that while I don't have to have my book fully plotted out before I start, I really, really, *really* need to know where the story ends up and at least one big point in the middle because then I can write toward those.

I learned these things because I failed. That's how you learn what doesn't work — and how you learn what can work that you didn't think was possible. Your project may be a hot mess, but the form is there, even if not immediately visible. Ten thousand words at the beginning may need to be cut because that's not where the story starts, but there's a subplot you realize you want to add. A woman who'll be the heroine of her own story in another book makes only a walk-on appearance, just enough to make folks aware of her existence, but not enough to interfere with the main story. There are the footprints for how the love story begins, grows, and comes to fruition. I learned all of this because there are manuscripts in the back of the closet I usually forget exist.

Except when there are lessons I need to remember that I've learned.

NOVEMBER 25

Ink on paper is as beautiful to me as flowers on the mountains;
God composes, why shouldn't we?

— AUDRA FOVEO-ALBA

I love words on the page. What's more, I love words on the page I've put there. I enjoy watching the letters form on the screen, the click of the computer keys, the very satisfying increase of my word counter. Yes, I watch my word count while I work. When things are going well, it's encouragement to do just ten more words, or see if I can round the total count up. When things aren't going so well, it reminds me I can't just get up and walk away because there are words to write. I love ink on paper as well, seeing the lines fill up on a page. The only reason I don't write more by hand is because my mind almost invariably runs faster than my pen. Then you have to retype things into your computer. I was an administrative assistant for too many years; I hate having to retype things.

These are the tools of our trade. We scribble on the back of napkins, receipts, in the margins of printouts, sticky notes, little files on our computers, delightfully organized indexes...if our mind runs that way. We are writers. We *write*. Sometimes the way is hard and our goal impossible to obtain, but if we put one word on the page, then another, and another, it's a pleasure how quickly they add up. If you let your mind go and trust the words, it's amazing what flows from your fingers or pen.

Five more days, including a four-day weekend somewhere in there for many of us in the United States. "Family," I hear you cry. "Commitments!" Be selfish. Once everyone's fed, take five minutes, ten minutes, just for yourself. Get away from the madness for a little while and let yourself be whisked back into the world of your story. Set a timer if things are tight but take the time for yourself. You'll have added to your word count, and you'll feel better for the breather. Gird your loins, we're almost there.

And if you're traveling this weekend, be safe. You still have much to compose.

THANKSGIVING

Who does not thank for little will not thank for much.

— AUTHOR UNKNOWN

In the United States, we celebrate Thanksgiving on the fourth Thursday of November, a day to overeat, watch too much football, make bets on what family grievances will be aired and try not to strangle your relatives and/or in-laws.

Have your phone handy as you never know when inspiration might arise. One November, at a very large family celebration, I found myself seated next to one of my husband's cousins. As I typed away on the phone, the cousin leaned over to whisper, "If you're writing smut, I swear Mom will make the roof come crashing down." A pause. "Please tell me you're writing smut." That is so in the file of things to use in a future book.

It's also a day to pause and reflect on our blessings. No matter how desperate times may seem—and I have known some truly desperate moments in my life—if you dig deep, there is something to be thankful for. It may be a small thing; a warm, fluffy cat, a book which brings you joy, a movie running on television which makes you smile, the taste of a familiar dish bringing back memories of happier times. It might be big things; a roof over your head, making it through one more month with food on your table, a hand to hold for better or for worse. Whatever it is, be thankful and nurture that small flame of warmth in your heart.

For those of you with families, enjoy the warmth, mine any drama for inspiration if necessary, and you can try using the excuse, "I have to write my words!" if things become too much. (You have no idea how many times I've done just that.)

For those of you on your own, I wish you well. I've been there, too, and I know today and the weeks to come can be some of the darkest of the year in more ways than one.

Best to you and yours today and all the days through the year. If you're ahead on your word count on this day, reward yourself with another piece of pie.

AND THE DAY AFTER

Decisions are made by those who show up.

— AARON SORKIN

Here's hoping your Thanksgiving (if you celebrate) was a good one. Not too much drama—or, if there was some, hopefully the contretemps yielded some story inspiration. I once had a t-shirt which proclaimed "WARNING: What you do may appear in my next book." My mother-in-law asked me not to wear it to family gatherings as it made people (i.e., her) nervous. My response of "Good," was not appreciated.

We're now facing the last days of November and the frantic race for the finish. Whether yesterday was a good writing day for you or things went by the wayside due to family commitments, that doesn't matter. Today is a new day and it's time to get back to work and show up at the page. Behind or ahead, today is the day to recommit to what you're trying to achieve.

When we overeat on one day (like, say, Thanksgiving), it's easy to say that we've blown our diet and beat ourselves up—often accompanied by even more food—rather than acknowledge we didn't do as well as we would have liked, refocus and move forward. The same thing happens with writing. Something blows our schedule up, the words don't get done and instead of sitting down the next day and keep on writing, we feel as if we've lost the thread and there goes another day. Then another, and another—and then we feel so far behind, we can never catch up.

I've been there, believe me. That feeling is the double-edged sword of these challenges, because you're racing against the calendar. For those 30 days, we live and die by the word count we set back in October. Let me offer some advice at this point: Don't.

I'm not saying don't get your butt that chair and write. Absolutely do that, challenge or no. But don't let the word count haunt you to the point where you stop writing because it seems overwhelming. "But you said a couple of paragraphs back today was a day to recommit to what we're trying to achieve," I hear you cry.

Yes, I did—and what we're trying to do is write a book. Let the word count go if you must and focus on your story. The month of literary abandon ends when the clock ticks over from November 30 to December 1. Your book will still be there, waiting for you to continue writing.

No matter where you are in your manuscript, today is the day to recommit to writing your book, getting that first draft down while the fire is hot. Being applauded for finishing the challenge is nice, but the real prize is finding you have created something which didn't exist when you started scarfing the last of the Halloween candy. You're bringing a new story to life. That's a thing so many people say they'd like to do *yet never make the commitment to getting the words on the page.*

You made the decision to do this, so let's show up today. Here's to good writing.

NOVEMBER 26

Do not dwell in the past, do not dream of the future, concentrate the mind on the present moment.

— BUDDHA

This is the spot where life is most likely going to derail you. The holiday season has officially begun, and it's possible the demands on your time have grown enormously. Also, the finish line is so close, it's easy to feel itchy, to want to be done. *Now*.

Breathe. In. Out. Focus on the moment. Don't think about how many words you have left in total. Focus on how many you need to do today. Set a timer and focus on how many you can write in the next twenty minutes. When the twenty minutes are done, take a brief break and stretch— then try another twenty minutes.

The old joke asks, "How do you eat an elephant?" The answer is, "One bite at a time." That's how books are written.

We talk in large numbers that seem too big to accomplish: 50,000 words in 30 days, 1,667 words each day. And yet...

The goal is possible, but it is accomplished one word at a time. John Steinbeck once wrote, "When I face the desolate impossibility of writing five hundred pages, a sick sense of failure falls on me, and I know I can never do it. Then gradually, I write one page and then another. One day's work is all I can permit myself to contemplate."

I have that quote posted next to my monitor. It's there to remind me that whatever we do, it is accomplished one step —one word—at a time. Each word we write today is a word we did not have before.

Today, focus not on the deadline looming on the 30th, but on the work you're doing right now. Be in the present and embrace what your creativity gifts you with today. If you don't look at the big picture, don't let the enormity of it all freeze you in your tracks, then what you achieve may be larger than you expected.

NOVEMBER 27

The moments of happiness we enjoy take us by surprise. It is
not that we seize them, but that they seize us.

— ASHLEY MONTAGU

At this point, we probably either love our story or we wish
we could consign the thing to some dark circle of Hell.
November 30 is coming fast—too fast for anyone who's
struggling to make their daily goal.

Does the story that seemed so brilliant on November 1
seem dull and lifeless now? Are you wondering why you
ever thought this was a good idea? Been there, done that.
Every writer hates their work at some point.

If your story is sailing along brilliantly, you can skip the
rest of this entry. The moments of happiness have seized
you and that's what will carry you through. The rest of you?
Pull up a seat.

We've been working so hard for nearly four weeks that
it's easy to lose sight of why we wanted to write this story in

the first place. (We may have lost sight of why we wanted to write, period, but that's another issue. See "When the Well Runs Dry.") What we need to do is rediscover that spark.

Think back to when the idea first came to you. What was your reaction? Did it make you smile? Was there a sudden urge to rush to the keyboard **right now** and start writing? Did making notes on how this story should be shaped begin to consume you?

That moment was pure, creative happiness, something which tapped us on the shoulder and said, "Hello!" Writing can be a slog and I'm not a fan of waiting until the muse moves you, but there's no denying the moments when our mind tells us, yes, this is what we should be doing are the best.

Take five minutes. Think about what in this idea brings you joy. If you write out of order, write something touching on that. If you write linearly, try to bring an element of that joy into the scene you're working on.

All work and no play makes Jack a dull boy, and scene, sequel, scene, sequel, move from one key point to another can make a dull writer. Our creative muscles are probably sore from the work they've been put through these past weeks. We can't necessarily take a break today, but let's play however we can and see if some of those moments of happiness will come upon us unexpectedly.

NOVEMBER 28

You can have it all. You just can't have it all at once.

— OPRAH WINFREY

Funny, I keep telling my characters that. At this point, they're not particularly interested in listening. But they're in the middle of the book, so they do not know the pain which lies ahead of them, especially my male lead. He has no understanding of how out of his depth he is. Naturally this is going to cause considerable trouble, especially to the female lead, who is falling for him despite her instincts which tell her otherwise. ::cackles evilly::

Character torture. Gotta love it.

Three days left in this year's challenge, and we should be in the middle of angst now, happily torturing our characters as they move toward the climax of their story. No matter where I am in a book, I'm starting to be filled with this dreadful urge that I want it all done *now*. It's so close, I can taste it. Now the problem is to keep focus as we head into the home stretch, make certain we don't let our minds go leaping all over the place. I'm not writing in order, but I need to stay with what I'm currently writing on, so I don't miss something I wanted to get down on the page.

People want to know the "secret" for writing, and aren't amused to hear, "Butt in chair, hands on keyboard." They want some mystical wisdom that will let them finish a book in just an afternoon and then see it as an instant best-seller on Amazon. There are plenty of folks out there who are willing to tell you how to do that—for a price. I've got a few in my inbox.

By now, you know that approach doesn't work. You've got twenty-seven days of sweat and frustration under your belt, too much caffeine and moments of using the wordiest descriptions you can to help you make that word count. You've been doing the work—it's just that the work seems to be never-ending. Welcome to the joy of writing.

Books are written one scene at a time. No matter how hard we try, we can't write two scenes at once. Trust me on this one; I've been trying for years. Today, know you can have your win and your finished draft, but you can't have it yet and you can't have it at the same time you're trying to figure out the scene where your protagonist uncovers what the person who's been dogging him all this time is up to. Focus. And if you need a prompt, you can always borrow today's quote—it's not a bad lesson for characters to learn.

THE AGONY OF DEFEAT

Winning is great, sure, but if you are really going to do some-thing in life, the secret is learning how to lose. Nobody goes undefeated all the time. If you can pick up after a crushing defeat, and go on to win again, you are going to be a champion someday.

— WILMA RUDOLPH

We're almost at the end, and it's time to talk about the elephant in the room: you may be in a position where you're not going to make it. All around you, folks are gleefully announcing they've met their goals and you...are looking at a word deficit you know you can't overcome.

There are lots of reasons that can happen. Disaster strikes you and yours (I hope not). The day job ended up demanding far more of your time than you anticipated (sucks and I've been there). Your tech went "boom" (this is why you make backups; a lesson I learned the hard way). The tale you are telling is "broken" somewhere and you either kept slogging away, hoping you'd find the answer, or you didn't realize something was wrong until way late in the game, and there's not enough time to correct your course.

It's a horrible feeling because the nasty little voice inside your head, the one that always shows up when something goes wrong, is having a field day now. You feel like you've failed, that this is just another thing you've tried and can't pull off.

Unless you completely blew off the writing and only remembered you said you were participating in a challenge a few days ago, I don't think you've lost. You have more words now than you had before you started. You made *progress*. Even if you aren't going to cross the finish line, you've pushed yourself outside your normal comfort zone and learned things.

At this point, you can keep writing these last few days and add some more words to the pile. I hope you will. Even if the momentum isn't enough to break the 50,000 word barrier, if you keep writing, you will keep that momentum going. That's what finishes the first draft, keeping at it.

If, however, you've reached a point where all of this has stressed you out so much that you simply cannot deal with the thing or you'll get even more stressed out, stop. You're not quitting but taking a break. Okay, so you won't finish this month. Allow yourself a day, two days, but no more than four days, then get back to work. Maybe the break will do you some good and you'll start work again with a fresh perspective. Look over what you've done. If there's a problem, maybe now you'll see the solution. Stand up again and keep moving. That's how you win the next time or the time after that.

Yes, the moment you realize you are not going to make

50,000 words sucks big time. Just know that this is not the end. It's a pause. Take the break and fill the well. Read, go out to dinner, throw yourself back into what stimulates your imagination. Make yourself strong so you can run the race again.

WEEK 4 WRAP-UP AND LOOKING AHEAD

This week...
- •We headed for the finish line.
- •Have you backed up your work?
- •Are you logging your words?

~

THE FINAL SPRINT...
- •Just two days left.

SPRINT TO THE FINISH

The starting point of all achievement is desire.

— NAPOLEON HILL

NOVEMBER 29

Maybe some stories are so good...so powerful...so wanted...that the Universe believes them. So good they're magic. So good they come alive.

— "LOKI: AGENT OF ASGARD" BY AL EWING

Two days left. Come the morning of December 1, this challenge will be behind us, win or lose. Today, though, we write. We write because that's what we set out to do, reach the goal we set by the end of November or get as close as we possibly can. A lot of folks have already hit their goals and stopped because that's what they wanted. Finished story or not, they wrote their words and that's enough for them.

If you're reading this, you're either a) still frantically trying to reach your goal or b) your story's not done yet.

What's more, you know it isn't done and you know it likely won't be by the end of day tomorrow, no matter your word count.

For a lot of people, the doing of the thing is enough. They've always wanted to take a shot at writing, and this month has given them an opportunity to try. A good deal of social life for these challenges revolves around coffee shops or online work sessions, the chance to be one of those people typing away on something that is obviously not school or work. There's nothing wrong with that and if the doing of the thing is what makes you happy, do the thing and enjoy. Writing is first and foremost for yourself; there's no other reason to go through this torture otherwise.

For those looking beyond the finish line to what comes next, take heart. You're not alone. Writing isn't just thirty days in November; it's a calling to tell the stories inside you.

Imagine not knowing where rain like that came from, or why or if it'd ever stop. Imagine how scary that'd be. For you and everyone around you—the highest chieftain to the littlest child. And imagine...just for a second, just imagine...you had a magic that could take that fear away.

The words, of course, are ones every storyteller knows well: *Once upon a time...*

Both quotes today are from *Loki: Agent of Asgard* #17, written by Al Ewing, art by Lee Garbrett, colors by Antonio Fabella. I recommend the series, but I highly recommend this issue even if you're not a comics fan. It's a wonderful meditation on stories and the power they hold and have always held.

Stories can change the world, because they present an idea that sparks the imagination of those around us or fills a need we didn't know we had. They can be, as Loki says, magic.

We're almost home. Let's make some magic today.

NOVEMBER 30

Victory belongs to the most persevering.

— NAPOLEON BONAPARTE

We're here. Thirty days and however many words you've written, if you're still pounding the keyboards, you've done good. Make no mistake; choosing to attempt a goal such as 50,000 words in 30 days is a long road, one I think is worthwhile because the point is *doing* the thing, to take time during the middle of the madness of November to make time for your writing.

I've lost a few of these since I began doing this annual challenge. I've always counted myself a winner, though. Each year teaches me something new, most often something I need to change or watch for, habits I've slipped into that actively work against the writing. The stress and heat of the moment that comes with committing to the month exposes cracks I didn't know were there. I walk away with a few "do this, not this" and some "you *must* change this."

There's a prize I've gained from over twenty years of November writing: I draft faster. I remember a time when reaching a thousand words a day was a struggle, a goal I didn't make more often than not. More recently, I've done sprints where I've made a thousand words in 30 minutes. I've consistently hit word counts of 2,500 in a day, and 3,000 and above is not unheard of. This carries over into the rest of the year and when I sit my butt down in the chair and focus, 1,667 words in a single day no longer seems so impossible.

Don't let those numbers discourage you; that speed didn't come overnight. In fact, trying to reach the mystical 1,667 each day nearly killed me the first few years. But steady application of the lessons I learn in this cauldron helped me to slowly, over time, increase my drafting speed. After a decade, if I can't break a thousand words on a given day, I have to ask myself what is wrong.

These are the gifts such challenges bring, win or lose. Proving to yourself you can find the time to sit your butt in the chair and write. That you can write more words in a day than you thought possible. Maybe you didn't win this year, but if you take the lessons you've learned over the past 30 days and bring them to your writing until November 1 next year, you'll do better. If you did make your goal, those lessons can help you write more words next year.

VICTORY IS OURS, *even if it isn't the obvious one. What have you learned this year?*

DECEMBER

What we think, we become.

— BUDDHA

DECEMBER 1—THE HANGOVER

My brain hurts!

— THE GUMBIES (MONTY PYTHON'S
FLYING CIRCUS)

Did we really just do that? Did we really just sit down and attempt to write 25,000, 50,000 words or more in 30 days? Did we worry about making our daily word count? Did we sneak in writing time whenever we could, including a few places we would normally never consider?

Welcome to December and the Writing Hangover. For the first time in 30 days, we awake without the dreaded word count hanging over our heads. We didn't race to the keyboard and start pounding away, squeezing in every word we could in the time we managed to carve out of our day.

And, like I do almost every year, I find myself missing it.

Writing is generally a solitary profession. I natter to my husband about my plot and characters, and he has been known to locate plot holes directly in front of me I've somehow missed—but when I sit down at the keyboard, it's just me and the voices in my head wanting to be let out. I spend a fair amount of time in the evening holed up in the office working on the current project in November, coming out only for dinner or the few TV shows that are absolute viewing for us. I have a writing partner I work with several mornings a week, but there's still a great deal of time on my own. Except for November. For 30 days, there are write-ins and word sprints, and the very act of writing becomes social because you're on Facebook or Discord or whatever service not to mess around, but to get writing done or you're at a write-in or...you get the picture. It's one reason I love this madness, even with Thanksgiving in the mix. And it's helped me. In 2015, I finished November with 76,186 words, a personal best and a speed I never would have even dreamed of before a friend told me about this craziness and I decided to give it a try.

RECLAIMING YOUR LIFE

You can have too much of a good thing and even though I miss not having words I absolutely need to write, I also feel the need of a break by the time December rolls around. I like having days where I can commit to finishing the sleeve on a sweater rather than getting that extra 200 words done. I want to catch up on the television I missed. I give up a number of these things in November and it's time to take them back.

What did you put aside during the last month that you've missed doing? Pick something and let yourself just have fun for a day. No, laundry does not count. Take a breath. Go for a walk with your loved ones. Hug your cat.

Writers do not live by writing alone. Our stories find their inspiration in the world around us—which means we need to be a part of that world. That means we need to leave our keyboards from time to time and live our lives because that's part of our writing journey. You've just spent a month burning an incredible amount of energy; time to refill the well.

RECLAIMING YOUR WRITING

"Uh, didn't we just spend a month focusing on our writing?" I hear you say. "Why do we need to reclaim it?"

Because these challenges are not how you are normally going to write. Try to write that fast for an extended period of time, you'll burn yourself out. This is a marathon, not a sprint. Pace yourself.

For 30 days, you made writing a focus. Even if you didn't hit 50,000 words, you learned how to fit writing in. You saw what your roadblocks were. Now that you're back to "normal" life, time to make use of that knowledge.

If writing is what you want to do, if this is more than just a one-time experiment, use what you've learned as the tools to make "words on the page" a major focus in your day-to-day life. Yes, you gave up things, chose to write instead of following those pursuits. Think about what you didn't miss over the past month that you stopped doing (or severely cut down). If you can find one or two things that you feel good about cutting out or devoting less time to, that's time you can devote to writing and revision. (Trust me, what you wrote needs revision.)

The question now becomes not, "How do I find the time to write every possible moment that I can?" but "How do I do this every day? How do I make this a part of my regular schedule?"

It's quite likely you've hit your desired word count and are nowhere near the end. Don't stop; keep writing—but at a level where you don't feel quite so frantic. Carve out a bit of that time you found during November and add words every day. Get yourself into a rhythm you can maintain without straining yourself. Don't worry if you're producing fewer words than you were a week ago. You'll get faster over time.

If you're within shouting distance of the end, you might want to push for the next few days. If it's going to take you more than four or five, though, I recommend going the slower route.

If you've finished your book, congratulations. Now put it in a drawer and don't look at it until after January 1. You need the time and distance before editing begins. Do **not**, under any circumstances, throw a cover on the thing and put it up on Amazon. Tempting as it might be, you're not ready. No one is after the heat of that crucible. There's a reason they're called "shitty first drafts."

Whether you're done or you're still typing away, let your mind wander to new ideas. Time to start thinking about what's going to come next.

After all, you only have eleven months until we start this madness all over again.

WHAT NOW?

I hope you've let a little time pass before you read this part. You've slipped back into the regular routine, though hopefully writing has become a part of that. The end of the year draws nigh, and the time is upon us where we make our goals and wishes for the coming year.

This is where we part company for a while and you find your own way. I hope you're finishing the journey you began in November with your story. If it's done, I hope you're working at a new one. Writing is a muscle; the more we exercise it, the stronger it becomes. Above all, I hope you had a good time. No, it wasn't all puppies and sunshine (and don't believe anyone who says it was), but when you look back, you will hopefully say, "I'm glad I did that."

What now? That's up to you. Revise and submit. Revise and publish. Realize it didn't work and put the manuscript in the proverbial drawer, then move on to the next thing. Think about what you learned over those 30 days and how you can put that knowledge to use. Know that there are always more lessons to learn. Challenge yourself. Be daring.

Above all, enjoy the journey.

We are such stuff as dreams are made on, and our little life is rounded with a sleep.

— WILLIAM SHAKESPEARE

RESOURCES AND OTHER THINGS

Before we part, just a list of a few things I think might be useful. These are resources that have helped me over the years, so I'll pass them along. This list is by no means definitive, but a personal compilation.

No Plot, No Problem by Chris Baty — Written by the founder of NaNoWriMo, this is a great look into how the original Novel November is "supposed" to work, along with some tips and encouragement. Chris has also recently started NaNo 2.0, which is filled with links and resources for the November novelist. He is *not* trying to replace the old NaNoWriMo site, and there are no interactive features. He does, however, link to several useful word counters, printable, digital, and spreadsheets.

Goal, Motivation and Conflict by Debra Dixon. Deb's book has been considered an essential work on the building blocks of story for, well, I don't think I want to date either of us that way. Long difficult to get, it's now easily available in eBook format.

On Writing by Stephen King—I find the back section where he discusses his vision of what a story is and how you should work at your craft encouraging and something I turn to when I need to get back to basics.

Bird by Bird by Anne Lamot. If you read nothing else in this, read the essay on "shitty first drafts." It helped me get over the idea that everything had to be perfect before I moved on. (Especially useful if you write by the seat of your pants.)

Story Genius by Lisa Cron — **Do not start this during November!** It's quite possible you could derail yourself completely. However, useful for the pre-Novel November prep.

THERE ARE numerous writing groups on platforms such as FB and Discord. A good writer's group is like gold. One that regularly makes you feel worse after they meet or actively hampers your writing? That's a sledgehammer to the knees. It may take a while to find a good fit, and don't be afraid to walk away from a group you don't feel works for you. Always protect your writing and your creativity.

This does not mean "no criticism." Refusing to accept criticism can be just as bad as letting someone belittle and demean your work—and going back for more. Both stances do not encourage growth. Keep searching for the happy medium.

ACKNOWLEDGMENTS

You can do anything as long as you have the passion, the drive, the focus, and the support.

— SABRINA BRYAN

Man does not live by bread alone, nor does a writer finish a book and bring it to market without helping hands along the way. I've been fortunate to have many on this journey, even if this lists only a few.

My friends on Dreamwidth, Facebook, and Tumblr through the years, many of whom have watched as I've gone through this challenge for over two decades. My friends on LiveJournal, now sadly scattered, who first said, "Hey! I heard about this thing!" My fellow WriMos through the years, both online and in person, and everyone who "liked" one of my November posts or tweets. Never discount the power of a simple "like."

Thank you to my original betas, Concavepatterns, Dettoit, and Lady of Midgard, who picked over the manuscript and caught typos, offered formatting suggestions and assured me I wasn't completely insane for doing this. My beta for this edition, Julie Johnson. Thank you for the lovely words of encouragement, as well as your work over the years in shepherding writers through November. Your Monday and Thursday "Morning JuJu" sessions helped keep me going when my world narrowed due to caregiving and health issues.

My parents, Richard and Gail Kinkead, who, so many years ago, told me "Why don't you try?" when I said I could tell a better story than the TV movie we were watching—and who gave into my pleadings for an IBM Selectric typewriter to replace our old manual. Miss you both and wish you could hold this in your hands.

Lastly, my thanks and love to my husband, Fred, who's put up with these fits of November madness, both win and lose. He moves our household's schedule around my writing each year, shoos me back to the keyboard and knows when it's time to take a break. This book would not have crossed the finished line without him.

— Caro Kinkead
Los Angeles
October 24, 2025

ALSO BY CARO KINKEAD

JUST A TOUCH OF SCANDAL (HISTORICAL ROMANCE)

The Accidental Viscountess

To Lure a Lord

Seasons of Love

CONTEMPORARY ROMANCE

Will You? (Kindle Unlimited)

ABOUT THE AUTHOR

As a child, Caro Kinkead was told Dr. Seuss' job was "writing books," and decided that was her goal when she grew up, along with being a ballerina, an actress, an archeologist and about a dozen other things. A fear of snakes signaled the end of her ambition to find the next Tutankhamun's tomb, the dancing and acting didn't quite pan out, but the love of writing remained, allowing her to enjoy those varied careers and more in her imagination.

Born and raised in Houston, TX, Caro grew up in a family of readers, where she developed a love of science fiction and fantasy thanks to her father, and old movies and the art of costuming from her mother. These days, she and her husband share a home in the Los Angeles area with their cats, a sizable book collection, and more yarn than she'd care to admit to.

If you'd like to about upcoming books or other news, you can visit her website at CaroKinkead.com and sign up for her newsletter. Which she sometimes remembers she has.